11/12/2017

Pastor Jim,

Adam and Eve
for Atheists

Thank you for the warm
welcome when I was a
guest in your Weippe
Church. And thank you for
your book.

Fred R Kuester

Fred R. Kuester

ISBN 978-1-64028-863-8 (Paperback)
ISBN 978-1-64028-865-2 (Hard Cover)
ISBN 978-1-64028-864-5 (Digital)

Christian Faith Publishing, Inc.
296 Chestnut Street
Meadville, PA 16335
www.christianfaithpublishing.com

Printed in the United States of America

The inspiration for this message is my father, Fred Albert Kuester. Dad was an atheist. He is dead. Totally dead. He was a good man. Don't cry. I've already taken care of that.

Table of Contents

The basic theme of this treatise is from St. Paul's First letter to the· Corinthians, Chapter 13, Verse 12

> For now, we see through a glass darkly but then face to face. Now I know in part, but then shall I know even as also I am known.

Adam and Eve for Atheists

There are many sincere people who have rejected the Gospel because some of the Old Testament conflicted with their perception of rational thought. Surely, there is a way to reach some of them with the saving message of Jesus Christ. We do have things in common to capitalize on in polite discourse. Instead of being a sticking point, the substance of the Adam and Eve story can become one item of commonality.

And where this commonality can be extended might help lead them out of their situation of eternal hopelessness.

I guarantee that the substance of the Adam and Eve story is agreeable to any individual regardless of the state of his faith or lack of it. Our presentation must not be lecture. We must also listen. In some situations, the atheist may feel the presence of our living God. That is one of our prayers.

Consider some simple truths of common agreement among all people: I will start slow and easy with an absolute, irrefutable fact. We come from dust as the Bible says. We will eventually return to dust as the Bible says. Too easy? Well bear with me Read the lessons of our title.

Two people. Adam and Eve. Male and female. According to the story, they lived in a beautiful, productive garden. All of their needs were generously met. Food, shelter, and companionship. She had a magnificent hunk of a man to follow around. He had a stunningly gorgeous, naked woman to follow him around. Could you live with a deal like that? Well probably.

They were not content. They had everything any normal persons could ever need or want, but there was one thing denied to them. The delicious fruit of a tree that wasn't theirs. I will call it a pear for purposes of this essay. They stole the pears. They became thieves. We have all known of people who were never satisfied with their lots in life no matter how richly they were blessed. Some of them complain. Some cheat and steal. They steal from their employer or from society or from their neighbors or their relatives. Some even steal from God. They dishonestly steal to enhance their financial or social position before they unhappily return to that dust. *Lesson #1.*

Then Adam and Eve hid from the owner of the pear tree. God said, "Where are you?" They answered and said, "We were hiding because we were naked."

So now they lied. They were hiding because their crime had been discovered. It is standard practice among thieves. They lie. They live in fear of discovery. They don't want to go to jail or lose their jobs, their families, or their friends if they have any. But if they keep at it, they are usually caught and punished. The jails are full of thieves. This behavior and its consequences continue to this day. It is written: "Thou shalt not steal." *Lesson #2*

Like most thieves, Adam and Eve were caught and convicted. *Lesson # 3*

Now what? You have read it in the papers. You have seen it on television. They blamed someone else for their personal crime. Adam accuses Eve. "The woman persuaded me to do this." Try this approach if you ever stand before a judge. You will get the same answer that Adam got, "No, Adam, you did it. Take responsibility for what you have done. There will be consequences." *Lesson #4.*

Then Eve piped up. "This snake in the grass persuaded me. It is this snake's fault." Same answer from the judge.

Then, now, and forevermore. Peer pressure is not an acceptable excuse. *Lesson #5.*

That is five modern day lessons so far. There are five more.

The greatest punishment was reserved for the lying ring leader portrayed as a snake. As the leader of this criminal enterprise, he had the book thrown at him. It is the same in the courts of today. The leader gets the greatest punishment. Lesson#6

Among other things, the snake lives in fear of the fiery tempers of women to this day. Snakes (criminals) generally come out at night when they are not easily observed. They are colored to blend with the black of night. The evil leaders of the world must constantly watch their backs if they are to preserve their own lives. Such leaders might assert that they wouldn't have done it but these people persuaded me. The blaming goes up and down the line. *Lessons #7 and #8.*

Adam and Eve lost big. But here comes the good part. We worship a merciful and forgiving God. God did not abandon them when he sent them out into the cold cruel world. He even made clothes for them out of animal skins. I perceive them as dressed in beautiful, warm furs. *Lesson #9*

All was not lost. They were ready to get on with their lives, but their lives were now more difficult. It is kind of like getting out of jail. Life is more difficult than if there had never been any jail time. *Lesson #10.*

The lessons are simple. The Hebrew Bible truly is the inerrant word of God. Everything is written for a purpose. For literal readers, both the history and substance are precisely accurate. Equally devout readers focus on the message and regard the history and science as not necessarily precise. A reasonable purpose being that the sixth century purpose was to get those Hebrews who wanted go, to get out of Babylon.

The best of both worlds is when proponents of either perspective respect each other. Disagreements in this regard are not personal Salvation issues so little if any personal harm is done either way

Even so there are some things that must not be compromised. Christians believe there is an afterlife. There is a God in charge of that afterlife. Jesus Christ is God the son of God. His mortal life was killed. He was raised from the dead. He lives and reigns forever.

Suppose the sincere atheist concedes the validity of the substance of the Adam and Eve messages but he challenges you like this, "Try me one more time if you can." This can be tough. Most Christians are not Bible scholars. I certainly am not. But here is another easy one that might impress your science minded friends. Genesis 1:9–10. The land appeared and separated from the waters. The inspired author gave us the first description of continental drift. How do we suppose the author of Genesis conceived the concept of continental drift? He had no telescopes, no microscopes, no GPS, no depth finders, no magnets, no Geiger counters, no seismographs. Just the inspiration of our God. Scientists did not accept the fact of continental drift until about 1960. Thousands of years later. If only the scientists would have had a little more faith.

For them and for all others: Christ is risen. He is risen indeed…

Preview
of Coming Attractions

I realize that I presented continental drift in a cavalier manner. We can get back to that later.

But first things before later things

Does God even exist at all? Or are all of the biblical stories products of the yearning minds of men? Do we accept God's existence on faith. I say, "NO." Many have tried that. It doesn't always work. People want evidence, solid evidence. Well, what is that?

Evidence is proof that something has happened or that something exists. I have evidence. I have facts that satisfy me. God is real. God does exist. Remember that this is written for atheists. There is little effect from presenting the messages of Jesus if people reject the very existence of God. So now I attempt to present an outlook of faith with facts that people may accept the reality of God. So please pray for the success of this attempt.

Do we see God in a gorgeous sunrise? Some people say they do. A sunrise does not prove the existence of God. Maybe so but not proof. Well, then, how about the even more spectacular sunset? Same deal. Not proof. Well then again, the flowers, the birds, the animals, and the fish; still not proof. These can generally be evaluated by natural processes. "Generally" means to me: How could this possibly happen without God playing a role? When and how often did God kick in? I truly believe he did and he does. Consider the complexity of DNA, its transcription to RNA and the RNA to protein. Study these and you will doubt your doubts. But again, no proof.

Are we impressed by rain when we need it or snow when we want it? No proof here. Not good enough.

Well, then, earthquakes, tidal waves, and forest fires; "surely" the powerful hand of God. There is plenty of evidence for "surely not." These are definitely not evidence of the powerful hand of God

But I declare to you that God does exist and he intervenes in our lives in special and wondrous ways. He does much more than merely exist.

For proof, we must dig deeper. How about the billions of stars moving at the speed of light but appearing ordered and organized? No proof here.

What could possibly be left? Not the weak force, not the strong force, but a wonderful cascade of rare events. A rare event can be defined as something that is so unique it cannot be evaluated by any statistical system.

We may someday have to apologize for our ignorance and our doubts, but these doubts are permitted. Where is God's role? Where did he kick in?

We will not persuade many atheists by reasoning our way through the mysteries of creation and crediting it all to God. We need more. But what is left after all of these concessions? They really aren't concessions. God may have been fully engaged in all of the above, but there is no irrefutable proof. We have none.

So where do we look next? I look for rare events in my own life. I avoid all science. I avoid the nature of the Earth, the nature of the Earth's organisms, and the nature of the universe. I evaluate the probability of events using mathematics wherever that approach seems reasonable. Don't be frightened. You will like this. You will be able to do these probabilities yourself and you will have a good time doing it.

But first, I will try to establish some level of credibility with you. I do have some science-mathematical credentials. I have been certified to teach math, sciences, and psychology at the high school level. Thus, as a firm advocate of the "scientific method," I am quite hard to persuade regarding the relevance of isolated events. When enough isolated events affect my life favorably, and I reflect on them, I know beyond a shadow of a doubt that God is on my side. Sometimes, I become aware after some reflection, that apparently unfavorable events also benefit me.

So to me God is very real. He has proven himself to me many times. I have no need of untested faith. I have facts. I am not guessing. God is real.

Next and Now:
God Life Stories

I will present some anecdotes of events
that have helped shape my faith.

God.
Life Story Number One

· ·

I married a farmer's daughter named Lena Mitchell fifty-seven years ago. As a young man, I was naturally attracted to her wit and to her intellect. She also had a great singing voice. All of the things that a young man sniffs for. In addition to these qualities, she was and is gorgeous etc. She will enjoy these observations.

Her father, Big Bill, was a no nonsense logger, farmer-rancher. The old curmudgeon wasn't impressed with my superlative qualifications. He figured she could do much better if she would deploy her feminine skills and her methods of persuasion more craftily. I figured she was crafty enough. The old gentleman refused to attend our wedding to give his last little daughter away. Her mother was there crying with delirious happiness. I felt a need to impress Big Bill and got my chance to do just that a couple of weeks after the wedding. They lived in a somewhat decrepit house. A large beam of expensive wood had rotted off of the foundation and the house was beginning to settle into the muck and mire of the mountain meadow that they called home. Here was my opportunity to come to the rescue. I would help him replace that crumbling beam if he would only help me pick it up.

We removed the old rotten beam and Big Bill prepared to measure the new expensive beam to size so it would fit in the old beam gap. I saw no need to measure because I thought any random length would work. So I showed Big Bill what I could do. I took the chain saw while he was choking on his tongue and I cut off a large chunk of this expensive beam. I cut it into two pieces. It turned out that a precise measurement within one-quarter inch was required.

No one was particularly happy at this point. There was no reasonable way to reattach these two inexpensive chunks. Our living God to the rescue. One of those chunks did fit precisely. I didn't get any thanks but at least I didn't get any old-time cowboy invective. Big Bill was a master of cowboy invective. I even got to buy the beer. I am a Lutheran. Lutherans drink beer as needed.

I later computed that I had to make that cut within a two foot long section to be within one-quarter of an inch of precision. There are ninety-six one-quarter inch spaces within a two-foot section. Therefore I had one chance in ninety-six of getting it right. Did God guide my hands? I am persuaded that he did, but I have proved nothing yet. I did have that one percent chance of getting it right.

We proceed through more of this prose I hope my motive will be clear. There are crucial events through which God sometimes chooses to guide our hands, our thoughts and our steps. He does these things for his purposes. His purposes are not always apparent to us. Sometime, he does give us guidance and assistance whether we know we need help or not. Sometimes, we recognize the help immediately; sometimes, it takes years; sometimes, we never know. And then again, we are expected to do our share; To learn as we go, to make our best effort to help ourselves, and to get things right on our own knowledge and effort. He does expect our gratitude for the training he has helped us get. Some of that training comes from making our own mistakes. Trust in the Lord, accept his instructions, and those mistakes will not leave us with insurmountable difficulties. So run the good race; fight the good fight; accept the Messiah(Jesus). Our final reward will be in heaven.

God.

Life Story Number Two

◦ ◦

This is Also a Carpentry Story

Lena, the crafty one, and I were teaching school at Akutan by the sea in the Aleutian Islands. Akutan is the home habitat of numerous bald eagles. The habitat is not too cold. There are no trees so food is easy to locate and the people of the village leave these noble birds alone when they fly into town.

Eagles are not always noble birds. Two of their favorite foods are house cats and small dogs. We "owned" a house cat. She was Lena's warm cuddler when the snow was deep and the wind was blowing at gale force. These were times that life in the village lost some of its charm. For more details, I refer you to some of the fishing shows on television.

Our apartment was situated up an open flight of stairs above the village post office. The creaky wooden stairs had open risers. Carpentry wood is scarce in this area.

I didn't observe this next scene personally but this is how it was described to me.

Lena was standing with her feet planted on the ground with her cuddle cat hunched between her feet. She was wildly swinging her broom at a large female eagle that was determined to have a supper of raw cat. I'm not sure how the people knew it was a female eagle but some of those Aleuts do have very good eyes.

Lena swung hard and scored a direct hit. The eagle flew away and the day was saved. I have always perceived this as a scene that could have come from the *Wizard of Oz*. I don't know about the "Oreo" part, although I did call it her riding broom from then on. We are still married.

Alright, okay, she fights off American bald eagles with brooms, but where do God and carpentry fit into this scenario? We are getting to it.

In the summers we would leave the Alaskan island and go to the Lower 48 to recharge our internal batteries, visit friends and family, get hairdos, new sacks of makeup, new high-heeled shoes, and other essentials to prepare for the next Alaskan winter.

But we would leave the cat. An eagle knew where the cuddle cat lived. And broom lady was gone. Kitty didn't have a chance. Crafty Lena came up with an idea from Oz or some other sinister place. My mission was to find some boards in some unspecified place on this treeless island. Then I could cut them to neat little pieces somehow and make neat little cubbies as risers between the treads of the open steps to our apartment. "That shouldn't be too hard" even though the nearest hardware store is hundreds of miles away by sporadically functioning airplanes. The cat could hunker in these cubbies when the eagle came to town.

Good idea. I did find some boards of random lengths. I measured the necessary dimensions by eyeballs and foot lengths. A saw was available. I didn't feel a precise fit was important and truly it wasn't. But it mattered to the maintenance man. When he came to inspect my work, he was flabbergasted. How could this be? Every thing fit well enough. The cat lived. The eagle had to go fish.

The odds of this measurement process passing the surprise inspection were probably about one in ten or some such thing. Again, something guided my hands when I cut those boards. Not just anything something. Give credit where credit was due. It was God.

What does this prove? Not much but we are getting there.

God.
Life Story Number Three

I hope you liked the first two life stories. Here is another carpentry experience. My neighbor, Dave, was doing some innovative fencing to keep his wandering sheep in a pasture where he could keep track of them. If a sheep finds a weak spot in a fence, it will be gone and the whole flock will go with it. A two feet wide sheep can somehow squeeze through a one foot wide hole. They can also jump, burrow, and perhaps call upon the forces of darkness to assist them in their *baaad* behavior.

This project contained a wide gate with an impressive overhead beam. He needed to attach some construction lumber to the poles supporting the beam. This was old, dried, case-hardened, super dried lumber that was almost impossible to drive a nail into. He was driving barn nails, but no matter, he had me to help him conform these nails to our will. We were using a smallish framing hammer and swinging it like a baseball bat with two hands. It would have been simpler and better had we drilled pilot holes first, but again, no matter. He had me to help him.

The job was going slow and I was getting tired. It turned out that we were going to need a shim. Dave went to get a shim while I continued to pound. I needed a short break so I stopped at three quarter of an inch of closure and waited for the shim. Normally, a shim is one quarter of an inch thick at its widest dimension. Here came Dave with a length of scrap lumber that was the exact thickness of the gap: three quarters of an inch. Unheard of. What could he have been thinking? No matter. It worked. We tapped it in and we were done. If I had closed the gap before I took my break, we would have had to open it again. That would have been very difficult. Praise the Lord and please forgive our imprudent comments of the moments.

Those who followed this whole story know there is no way under the sun that I could have made any of this up. Couldn't be done.

Perhaps this doesn't sound like much, but you weren't there; and truthfully, not all of God's help is for Earth shaking problems. I find much gratification in the smaller helps that happen all of the time. It's kind of nice to be reminded that God is always there. Hallelujah, because the forces of darkness will never go away either. It is humbling to reflect upon the numerous times that I took my cue from the dark forces. Remember the Lutheran Beer? We can all be humble in that regard. No matter how grateful we are for the sacrifices of Jesus as he suffered and died for our sins, our sorrow can never match his grace.

I will give the odds of this somewhat favorable outcome as one chance out of ten. As a matter of interest, the sheep never found a weak spot at this spot in the fence. They did find other escape opportunities but you knew that.

Before we proceed, this seems like a good spot for a probabilities discussion. How likely is it that something will happen and how often will it be likely to happen? The probability methods are subject to abuse and we don't want to do that. Even if we were inclined to prove our points with false analysis, it would be a very short interval until our falseness was discovered.

Here is a basic description of some probability analysis just to illustrate the point.

Look at a coin, it has two sides. You probably knew that already. If you flip that coin, there is a fifty percent chance that it will come up heads and a fifty percent chance that it will come up tails. Fifty percent means if you flip it one hundred times, it will come up heads fifty times. It's not a perfect system, but we won't worry about that now.

So your fraction is fifty divided by one hundred, which reduces to one over two.

Suppose you decide to flip the coin three times and you want to know the likelihood of three consecutive heads. You multiply one over two by itself three times. Your probability is one chance out of eight. Four in a row would be one chance in sixteen.

How can this be abused? In the three God life stories, I stated a probability. One chance in ninety-six, one chance in ten, and another one in ten. If I multiply these together, I get one chance in 9600. I could conclude that such a rare event could so seldom happen that I now proved that God existed. That would be delusional mathematics. Beware of people who use mathematics to prove their points regarding God. He is not amused.

So, as I stated, I have proven nothing yet. But I am sure getting the idea that as these God situations add together in my life and in the lives of other people that we have one big, wonderful, and powerful God. If you agree with that conclusion now would be a good time to send a prayer.

I won't try to estimate probabilities for any of the life situations in the next pages, although I do mention the concept now and again.

Now it gets a little tricky. I feel a need to describe some situations in a way that might seem a bit off topic to you. For that, I am tempted to apologize to you. I do apologize for resisting that temptation to apologize. I assure you that I will constantly be on topic even though you might disagree a bit. To console myself and you in our difference of opinion, I refer to an expression from my clever, crafty wife, Lena. You have met her before. She speaks thusly, "You can't expect me to agree with you every single time." That is a true fact. Sometimes, she gets kind of cheeky. Even so we have been married and have lived happily ever after for fifty seven bliss filled years.

We live near the enchanting village of Kamiah, Idaho. Kamiah lies on the banks of the Clearwater River in the depths of a two thousand feet canyon. The canyon is so structured that we can see to the very tops of the surrounding hills. It is important that you know this. The hills are covered with a blend of grasses, shrubs, and ponderosa pine trees that extend to heights exceeding one hundred feet. Intermingled with the slopes and the mixture of vegetation are farms, ranches, and groups of houses, and wooden outbuildings. I will get back to this Chamber of Commerce type of picture as we go long. Those of you who have ever lived in this type of geographical location are now persuaded that I have not strayed from the topic of praise, wonder, and gratitude for our God. It didn't take long, did it? Thank you for sticking with me so far. If you are ever in this area, stop in to visit if you have time. We are a friendly bunch who live at Kamiah, and there are lots of churches of many denominations. If you want a particular denomination we probably have it here. We worship Jesus, The Prince of Peace. No one is killing any one else because of their differing faith. I did digress a bit here, but I couldn't help it.

Now a bit of history and of the geology, geography and meteorology (weather). God may have put it all together. I will try. Up the rivers that flow toward our happy home, the canyons get narrower and their slopes get steeper, much steeper. The rivers come raging out of the high mountains. The variety of weather is controlled by the combination of mountain and canyon effects blended with an overriding warm westerly breeze. It gets complicated, but our weather forecasters do their best. So they claim.

Now for the bit of history that you have been waiting for. A little more than two hundred years ago, the explorers, Lewis and Clark, with a small band of men, one woman, one baby, one dog, and a small herd of horses arrived at the top of the "immense Bitterroot Mountains." They were at a dip in the hills at what is now called Lolo Pass, on US highway 12. The Lochsa River canyon loomed below. If you are a flatland person and you would seek a brief moment of adrenalin terror, I heartily recommend that you experience this view yourself. Although there are no toilet facilities at the bottom of the ensuing descent, the stories are many of terrified women who have bailed out of their cars to pee alongside the road when they reached the bottom. As one of them said, "I didn't care who saw my bottom." I cleaned that up a little bit, and I assure you that I am still on topic. Sometimes, the messages of God are strange and wondrous.

Lewis and Cark were apparently beyond feelings of terror at this point but they did know they were in trouble, big trouble. Their horses couldn't manage these steep, rock infested canyons. Neither could their own feet. But they had to descend. Snow covered hills were to their north and to their south.

Some of that variable weather mentioned earlier. Down they went.

Things went tolerably well for a few miles and then the terrain became impassible to any creature that wasn't a wild animal. Even the wild animals became scarce and the entire group came close to starvation a little further into the trip. They ate at least one horse to tide them over.

After those first few miles, they had to leave the canyon for the gentler ridges to the north. From the top of these mountains, their only view was more and higher mountains. These are the mountains from which our unpredictable weather originates. I promise to get to the horrors of some of that weather as we go along. I am still on topic, although it may seem convoluted to the casual observer.

And then from a high knob they could see, still many miles away, the rolling hills of the Weippe Prairie, the land of the Nezperce Indians. The prairie land extends to the hills above Kamiah. The weather there is different from our weather because of the two thousand-foot difference in elevation. If you drive about five miles in any direction up the hills, the weather changes. Sometimes for the better, sometimes not. The bottom line is, our weather comes from tangled knots of deep canyons, rolling prairies, high mountains, and variable winds.

Summary for Kamiah itself: Our weather is generally mild. Quite warm in the summer. Decent in the winter with very little snow (about six inches per winter by my unscientific, general observations). But you don't have to travel far and that can change fast. That changing weather situation is the crux of much of the God messages that follow. We can live or we can die by the conditions that our weather imposes upon us.

God.
Life Story Number Four

. . . .

We move from the life story of number three to this potentially deadly situation. At one time, I had a 100-mile trap line that extended from home to the headwaters of the Lochsa River. It paid some of the bills at times when we were very short of money for living expenses. Three kids and lots of medical expense.

US highway 12 is narrow and winding. The north edge of the road follows the base of the cliffs while the south side is perched above the river. There are no shoulders. For many years, prompt efficient snow removal was not achievable. There are respites from this treachery but the situation is generally as just noted. So we drove on a base of packed snow that was often too slippery for mortals to walk upon. I drove this highway two hundred miles every three days regardless of the weather from the balmy clime of Kamiah into the cold, deep snow in the mountains.

Common hazards were fallen rock, fallen trees, deer, elk, black moose, and incredible tourist behavior. Some sponge-brained pilgrims would stop on these dangerous curves to gawk at the abundant wildlife. They would even get out of there cars for better views and memorable photographs. I did work hard to maintain my sense of Christian charity.

Considering all of these road hazards, I am confident that my lovely wife is constantly grateful to God for my long life. How could it be otherwise?

My transportation was a pickup truck with many hard earned miles and three winters at the frozen tundra of North Pole, Alaska. My best guess is ninety percent of those miles were in situations like those just described.

One nice summer day, Lena and I drove one hundred miles on nice roads to deliver a boat to a grand daughter. We were driving on a nice stretch with wide shoulders and wide lanes through the wheat fields of the Palouse Prairie near Pullman, Washington. It was a nice trip until our motor blew up. That spoiled things. As I eased onto the wide shoulder, I heard my wife's prayer, "Thank you, Father." I, feeling an instant Spirit of gratitude, said something similar.

What was wrong with our minds? This makes no sense. Our vehicle blew up ninety miles from home. We were standing on the side of the road praising the Lord. Had we lost our minds or what passes for minds?

The odds were high that this catastrophe would have happened on a stretch of high hazard road at a time of great danger. Technically, it should have happened where there was no room to escape traffic on a narrow, slippery lane with no shoulders. Traffic would have been coming from both directions around the snaky curves. Even worse, it could have happened at night. Who knows what wrecks could have happened?

So did God enter the motor and cause it to blow up in that favorable spot? Absolutely not. He knew disaster was imminent and he did know the decrepit condition of the motor. He guided my thoughts to be in a safe place when the gaskets blew. The odds of an unguided safe landing were small. I am glad to give full credit to our God.

This gets even better. Normally, Lena is not with me when I drive, but she was with me and she had a cell phone buried in the mysterious maze of her purse. Without her, there would have been no phone because I didn't know how to use it. Luckily, she is somewhat more talkative than I am and she appreciates the opportunity to communicate at will. It is a concept that I do not understand. We have other such concepts. With that phone, she arranged for help and the rest is history. We are still living happily ever after. Praise the Lord.

God.
Life Story Number Five

· ·

How about a rainstorm that worked in my favor? Considering the obvious strength of my faith, you will probably be surprised and possibly distressed by an insight of mine. God does not control the rain storms or the lack of them. The rain comes as a natural result of cyclical meteorological processes. Now that you start to know where I am coming from, please read on. Sometimes, God intervenes in a special way.

This is about a horrible storm while I was checking my trap line. For humane considerations, trap lines must be checked with precise regularity. These are the rules. No exceptions for weather. These rules are strictly enforced by the state's professional Conservation Officers (Game Wardens), and these guys are good at what they do. Sometimes, I think they check my traps more often than I do.

So I headed out into the deluge, the wind-driven downpour. Not thinking clearly on this dismal morning, I didn't bring any rain clothes with me. Another cup of coffee might have helped. I did have a change of dry clothes to put on at the end of the day so I could drive home in a bit of comfort. This meant eight hours of being soaked in temperatures barely above freezing. The danger of hypothermia wasn't high level, but it couldn't be ruled out either.

So I came up with a plan. Why not bypass the first fifty miles of traps and begin checking at Fish Creek? Fish Creek is fairly big water It would be labeled as a river in lots of the country. Then I would check the traps along the upper stretches of the Lochsa, getting wet and miserable for only four hours. Change into dry clothes and drive comfortably back to Fish Creek all the while warming my suffering carcass. Then check the traps to home, freezing wet and shivering, but all the while getting closer to a warm bath and a hot meal.

That seemed like a good plan. Well thought out. Maybe Lena is training me to be crafty? Very smart. Never mind that I forgot to bring rain clothes.

Irrelevant.

So I drove through the driving rain for about fifty miles. The water was almost too much for the windshield wipers. If you have ever driven through Nebraska when it is raining hard, you know what I am talking about. One quarter mile from Fish Creek the clouds lifted, the rain stopped and the sun shone beautifully. I checked the fifty miles of upper river traps in dry comfort. I got to the end of the line, turned around, and drove back to the misery awaiting me from Fish Creek to home. When I got there, that rain had also ceased. The weather was balmy the rest of the way. I still took a warm bath at home. My wife prefers me to be not too stinky when I crawl into bed.

Now I ask you, do you think God regulated that rain just for me? No he didn't. He and I are close, but not that close. Of course, he knew where that storm ended and I firmly believe he planted the idea in my mind, "start trapping at Fish Creek." He took pity on me and I appreciate it to this day. This is a matter of significance though: I am expected to do my own remembering of rain clothes in the future. It is written, "Do not put God to the test." Look that up in Mathew. Jesus said it. You can find it.

I am persuaded that signs, large and small come to all who believe in the inward presence of our mighty God. He might come to non-believers also. I don't know. I have no opinion in that regard. It is easy to miss these signs. Also, it can be easy to recognize these signs if we are looking for them, but be careful. It is easy to let our imaginations run wild. God told me to do this. God told me to do that. People have murdered other people because they were persuaded that God told them to do it. God doesn't send these kind of messages. Jesus is the Prince of Peace.

Of the hundreds of times that I have driven this road that is the only time that a deluge like this has begun and ended in that place. Does anyone care to take a try at figuring the odds?

God.
Life Story Number Six

This is a goofy one, but very important to me. Along with trapping from a business perspective, I put in lots of time helping my rural friends who have problems with wild animals. People with fish ponds, irrigation ditches, and fruit trees are plagued by beavers draining with their burrows and by chewing down their trees; chicken and duck people are plagued by raccoons, mink, and skunks. Coyotes feast upon house cats, small dogs, and sheep. Muskrat burrows are a special problem at any type of pond. I help where I can.

This episode is about otters. These cute fuzzy creatures are a horrendous problem where people are trying to raise fish. Among other places, I am always welcome at fish hatcheries. Otters eat fish. Lots of fish.

An interesting side to this story is it also illustrates the problems of opiate drugs. I had a difficult, painful surgery a few years ago before the trapping season opened. The pain was controlled with hydrocodone. It didn't just control the pain; it also controlled my mind. I made many mental mistakes. Here is one.

When I read the trapping rules for the year I got seriously confused. Each year, we are permitted to trap two otters. I read the new rules as permitting the catch of three otters. A third grader could have done better. There had been no changes. Two otters were still the permitted catch, but armed with this lack of knowledge I set three otter traps at a fish hatchery.

I quickly caught two otters. The hatchery manager was with me when I caught the second one. I told him that I had caught two and would leave a trap set for the third one. So far so good and so bad.

I went home and turned on my computer to check my e-mail. One year before this, I had received a message from my friend, Doug, in south west Idaho that contained the otter rules for that year. I had not looked at that message for a full year. It stated that the limit was two. My thought was that this should have been updated to three for this year. I didn't give it much thought, but for reasons unbeknownst to me I took out the current rules and discovered my drug induced error.

So I hurried back to the fish hatchery and picked up the trap before it made another catch. It does surprise most people that we do set our traps for specific species. It's not a perfect system, but most of our catches are for targeted species. More fish of an endangered species did live to swim another day. I could have done more but rules are rules.

The amazing thing is I had gone a full year without opening that e-mail. Had I gone one day longer, I would have been in big trouble with the law because more otters were right there. What caused me to push that computer button right then? I had God's help working in my thoughts. I can't prove that, but this is "life story number six," and I am getting used to God's help. It is very humbling and I am very grateful. Why me Lord?

I will now describe three health situations where some mighty force has helped us enormously. I promise to avoid biology except for one healing aspect. The reason is that miraculous biological cures can be attributed to modem medicine or spontaneous remission. I am trying to present situations where the presence of a higher power could be recognized by the most confirmed skeptic. These next three defy any skeptic's scorn.

God.

Life Story Number Seven

· ·

This medical situation does have a healing aspect, but it is a minor aspect within a larger problem. The larger problem was not fixed, cured, or lessened at that time. My lovely wife, Lena, was in a hospital bed dying from the shock of excruciating pain that no medication was able to relieve. Finally, I left her there and drove thirty miles home to try to sleep.

Before I slept, I prayed something like this, "I am not asking for healing. I would appreciate the best possible result considering what you know of these circumstances." However, could you ease the pain to something tolerable? Maybe I should have had the confidence to ask for more. It was 10:30 P.M.

Before I came to the hospital the next morning, I called her on the telephone—land line. She said the pain was tolerable at an intensity of five out of a possible ten. It sounded good and it was. I drove to the hospital and asked her when the pain eased.

She said, "10:30." The time I had prayed. Lena didn't know about the prayer. As a bonus, healing proceeded nicely from this point. I regard that as a benevolent answer to a reasonable, non-presumptive prayer request.

As time went by, the source of the pain was located and somewhat fixed. It has never returned at that intensity. Maybe God would have cured her if there had been a major organ breakdown but why should he? With seven billion people in the world and average life expectances of seventy years one hundred million people die every year. Who should he choose? It seems a lot for me to ask for such special consideration. Others see it differently. My preference is to ask him to guide the hands and the wisdom of the doctors. So far, it is working. However, we look at it I am convinced that God played a role and most Christians will agree with that.

God.
Life Story Number Eight

⦁ ⦁

From our rural home, it is seventy miles to our dentist. He is a nice guy not withstanding his chosen vocation. His first name is Bill. We call him doctor bill. We are quite polite about it. After all he is a dentist. Dentists are not to be messed with.

Lena drove the beautiful but treacherous seventy miles to a Tuesday dental appointment at ten in the morning as I recall. She strolled into the waiting room at 9:55 just as another woman was drifting toward the back rooms of medieval devices that dentists stick into people's mouths. The ensuing conversation went like this:

Receptionist: "Good morning, Lena. Why are you here?"
Lena: "I am here for my ten o'clock. appointment."
Receptionist: "Your appointment is on Thursday"

Lena: (Sanitized version) "O! Shucky Darn!"

Actually, farmers daughters talk more plainly, more expressively than that and she was trained by Big Bill but you get the idea. She was seventy miles from home and Doctor Bill had no room for her. Moreover, she was going to have to make the same 140-mile round trip again on Thursday.

Lena: (Sanitized again) "O! Fooey."

The other woman: "My husband has an appointment here on Thursday. I would rather come on Thursday myself. Could I trade with Lena? She could take my appointment today. And I could take hers on Thursday."

Receptionist: "It's a done deal."

So what are the odds?

1. Confuse the date of the appointment. Actually pretty good. It happens once in a while but you didn't hear it from me.

2. Arrive on time. It happens quite a lot in fast drive situations when the highway patrol officers are taking their coffee and doughnut break.

3. How likely would it be that a perfect stranger would be headed into the treatment room just as Lena walked in? And that perfect stranger would have an appointment

for her husband at the same time as Lena on Thursday, and that woman would offer to trade.

The timing of this is truly unreal. If Lena had arrived earlier she would probably have left and never met the other woman. If she had gotten there one minute later, the other woman would have already been in the treatment chair with Doctor Bill preparing to pounce down into her mouth.

I regard this as a rare event with God managing the timing. There is no reasonable way to figure the odds. Only a joker would try. I tried but that can be our secret. This is a one-of-a-kind incident that defies human explanation.

God.
Story Number Nine

. . . .

I had an interesting and gratifying experience with a God-sent group of shuffling nurses. It was a Monday morning in our village. I knew that I needed to be 180 miles away in Coeur D Alene early Tuesday for an important medical appointment, but I couldn't go for certain procedures if I was sick.

It turned out that I was very sick this Monday morning. Our local clinic opens for doctor and nurse services at nine in the morning, but clerical help arrives at eight o'clock. When I am really sick, there is some comfort to being in a clinic even if the wait will be a long one, so I went in at eight o'clock with high hopes and low expectations.

Then I learned of the unexpected. The nurses and doctors weren't coming in. My first thought was of swinging parties on Sunday night. After all, this area has some vestiges of the Wild West even yet. We don't talk about it much except perhaps on rodeo weekends, but there had not been a swinging party. I don't know to this day where the doctors and nurses disappeared to. I am confident it can all be explained but perhaps not to me.

But I was sick, and the situation did resolve itself. The nurses were to be replaced for the day by nurses on call from Grangeville which is thirty-five miles away. On these roads, that is about a one hour trip. I suppose that in order to allow themselves some float time for the vagaries of travel, they had left Grangeville early and were already on the road. In fact they were on the edge of town. That was good because I wasn't getting any better.

I had barely sat down for what I thought would be a one hour wait when in came the nurses. They should have had a drum roll but that ceremony was skipped. I did get a highly professional evaluation and treatment by a nurse practitioner and two nurses. The regular nurses wouldn't have been there for another hour so. So I got more or less healed one hour earlier than I could have hoped.

I was able to keep my appointment in Coeur D Alene the next day, although I did have to drive through a storm in the dark because of a late start.

Never before have I seen a situation like this develop. Why did the visiting nurses leave early enough to get to Kamiah an hour early. I can only think that God guided their thoughts. Again, this was a rare event, an isolated event and there is no credible way to calculate the probabilities. The only thing I know for certain is God did it.

God in the Time of Fire.
Life Story Number Ten

The summer of 2015 was desperately dry in our Clearwater Valley. The hills were brown grass from the river to their very tops. The tops are the leading edge of the high elevation prairie. We had a series of lighting strikes and fires blazed all around. Since we live near the bottom of these hills, I felt reasonably safe. But there was no accounting for a ferocious wind that came roaring off of the prairie and sent the flames down the hills with the speed of a saddle horse. The wind driven fire came from all directions. One hundred-foot tall ponderosa pine trees became huge candle torches. It was spectacular.

The sheriff issued an order for mandatory evacuation of all residents, but he wouldn't force anyone to leave if they were foolish enough to stay. I told the deputy that I had done a lot of fire fighting and I thought I would know when it was time to run. Lena and I rejected the mandatory evacuation. We stayed, and many other residents did the same. Many of us have fire fighting experience in our back grounds. We take care of ourselves and each other when we can. About seventy-five houses burned. Also many barns and other out buildings. One house, about seventy-five yards from ours, burned. The wind driven heat was so intense that it was fully engulfed within seconds; not minutes, but seconds. Lena and I had fire on all four sides when we finally did leave. She decided that fire on four sides was fire on enough sides.

But I had done a lot of pre-suppression work; and though the flames came within twenty feet of our house, all we lost were a couple of cords of black locust fire wood that were in our north pasture. Five other houses in our general area didn't burn, but many outbuildings were lost. An equal number of the houses in our general area were lost along with all of their contents.

We live in a fire protection district but no pumpers came to help. We were on our own. We did have some small but important help from a traveling firefighter who stopped in his travels with a few gallons of water in a pickup truck. Lena asked one of the men from the fire protection district why we got no help. He didn't send help because our little area was regarded as hopeless. The terrain was wrong and the vegetation was wrong. He may have been right But we didn't burn.

So how does God fit into this desperate situation? Our house didn't burn. This is important. I must not give the credit to the grace of God. Here's why. If I were presumptive to do that then the many people who lost everything could say, "Where was my grace?" There is no way that I could imply that God favored me over them. Neither do I believe it. But I do believe that God did play a role. Thus, if a place could be defended and if people did do some pre-suppression work and if they defended while they could, then God extended assistance. And, without going into detail, that is what happened here. We did do the work and we did get a small amount of help from the fire fighter. A small amount but a very useful amount.

There is nothing like a strong wind to turn a manageable fire into a raging inferno. I recommend this experience to no one.

The fire I just described continued for many miles. The same fire burned toward our friend, Roy Pethtel's, ranch headquarters. Roy also rejected mandatory evacuation. The fire burned among his outbuildings and toward his house. It burned a hay barn containing three hundred tons of grass hay to the ground. It did not kill any cattle. They were out in the dust and the mud. Roy had done some pre-suppression. Plus, he did have professional help with pumpers, but he could still have lost it all. As it was, he lost plenty.

He had another hay barn filled with four hundred tons of hay. One of his helpers was walking a patrol route. There was a short path and a longer path. He paced back and forth on the short path.

Then on one tour for no apparent reason he took the longer path. He glanced up at the very instant that a flaming ember carried by the wind blew into this barn and ignited the hay.

It only takes a few minutes for such a fire to torch an entire barn. Because of that change in path and that quick glance, the fire fighters got right on that blaze while it was still small. They extinguished it with minimal damage.

That barn is adjacent to Roy's wooden garage and machine shed, and the machine shed is near the wooden house. Roy would probably have lost everything if that hay barn fire had not been quickly extinguished.

Roy is a devout Christian and an active member of the Gideons. He understands the concept of not touting God's grace among people who lost so much, but he insists that God played a role and I agree.

Why did his helper change his route of travel at precisely the critical moment? Why did he glance up at the precise instant that the burning ember blew onto the dry hay in the barn? GOD guided his thoughts. That is the only reasonable explanation.

Two of the reasons I cite these two fire stories are:

1. God's grace is always with us, but is often tempered by a situation that is beyond our understanding.

2. Be careful when claiming God's grace. People who were not so blessed at that particular time may reject God and you forever.

Adventure

. . . .

I earnestly hope that you are convinced, or at least somewhat persuaded, that there truly is a great and wonderful God. We will get back to that.

But first:

The publishers commanded of me just a little more. I am encouraged to write of adventures. As if direct contact with God in what I have already presented isn't adventure enough. I will obey for three compelling reasons:

1. They have the authority. I have always been a stickler for authority. Ask any one who doesn't know me very well.

2. They own the printing presses. This gives them an iron hand and steel tipped boots.

3. They have the check book. A minor item, but part of the authority package.

Somehow, I am expected to pull interesting adventure experiences from the clear, cold sky, all the while maintaining a God centered theme.

Surprise to them. I think I can do it if my typing fingers hold out. All both of them. Lena and I have had some interesting years both inside and outside of the house.

My hard working wife and I lived, worked, and played in Alaska for eight and a half years in the 1990s. There were three hazards at our locations. These were Fahrenheit temperature, Centigrade temperature, and water. Liquid water, snow, and ice. We lived at three separate locations. These were so widely scattered from each other that you couldn't get to any one of them from the others. Alaska is a big place.

The Adventure
in Akutan by the Sea

Akutan is an island bordered on the north by the Bering Sea and on the south by the Pacific Ocean. The Village of Akutan is on a narrow deposit of land in a sheltered bay at the eastern tip of the island. The waters of the two seas are of differing temperatures. This leads to calamities of weather. The winds have to be felt and seen to be fully appreciated. The wind effects on the ocean waters are gargantuan. But the people are friendly with a great sense of humor. As they say, "There are 90 people and two teachers living in this village." I like to imagine that we rose to the position of also being people during our four year stay.

One of our first talks went like this, "If you go out to sea in a boat, do not go out with white people. They will drown you. Go out with us. We will get you home." A few times, I had good reason to doubt that we would actually get home but they could do it. We always made it home.

Here is a neat story: Three of us went commercial halibut fishing in the standard eighteen foot aluminum boat that they declared was sea worthy. The night was pitch black dark when we shoved off the boat anchorage. We motored along for a while. Then our leader, Art, cut the motor to give instruction, "It's important not to panic." It was still blacker than Coaly's Black Labrador dog so I could see no reason to panic. I could see nothing. Art had just given me a reason to at least be nervous and it fixed in my mind.

So we proceeded to the fishing area at an unspecified spot in the unmarked sea which they were able to—find in the dark. It became my job to steer the boat. The two Aleuts baited hundreds of hooks with a couple of ounces of herring and we were fishing or I thought we were. It was still inky dark. My course of boat steering was directly toward a light off in the distance, but sometimes I couldn't see the light and I didn't know why. What I did know was I was steering with one hand while I was puking over the side from sea sickness.

It got light. The waves were six feet high and the boat had been climbing and descending them at all angles. That's why I kept loosing track of the light. Part of the time, I was looking straight down into the water. Part of the time as looking up at the black sky, and all of the while the boat was rolling. No one else puked.

We fished all day. At the end of the day, there was daylight at the do-not-panic zone. There was one huge, white capped, thirty feet high wave menacing over our heads. It seemed impossible but our little boat pulling a raft filled with 3,000 pounds of dead fish climbed that horrendous wave.

If you are ever drifting in the Dutch Harbor area, you would enjoy a visit to Akutan. My friends might even regard you as "people." Some kind soul might even offer you a ride in a boat.

Yukon River Adventure in Grayling

Grayling is a village of about 250 Holikachuck Indians. This is an area of deep snow and frigid cold. Forty degrees below zero is commonplace with extremes to about sixty below. It's possible to get used to minus forty, but minus sixty is dangerous. The ice on this part of the Yukon gets four feet thick. The Iditarod, ceremonial sled dog race goes through Grayling in alternate years.

When we weren't working in the school or preparing for classes, there were solitude opportunities such as cross country skiing and snowshoeing at thirty-five or forty below. The Natives were mostly intelligent enough to stay in their heated cabins at this time of year. Being a slow learner, I got out and explored the area. The town and forest was actually pretty well lighted by the Northern Lights for most of the winter, so night skiing could be enjoyable.

On a day of mental lapse I skied across the Yukon. I am the only one that I have ever known who has done that. Some claim to fame, huh? I felt safe. The ice was four feet thick. That is plenty safe for a moderate weight human even if he is driving a large truck. There were important things that I did not know.

Some of the residents noticed what I was doing. While I was gone, a couple of women came to our cabin. They were distressed and told Lena, "Don't let him do that again. We know this river and we drown in it. Fred does not know this river. Under the ice there are scattered inputs of warmer water that erode the ice. Some of these open water areas stay unfrozen in the, coldest of winter weather. There can be thin ice along the edges. Even worse, they can get a very thin skim of ice covered with a light dusting of snow on that ice. An ignorant white guy could easily break through into the cold unforgiving current of the Yukon."

I apparently made these people nervous with my exploring activity.

There are also belligerent moose and big, growly grizzly bears lurking close to town. My friend, Henry Deacon, asked me what should be done with my body if I died out there. I flippantly answered, "Just toss me in the river, Henry." Henry wanted a better answer.

Back to my foolhardy ski trip. Sure enough, just as predicted, I got to the eastern shore and there were several acres of open water. I didn't like it so I did maintain what I hoped would be a safe distance from the edge of this opening. After a little imprudent exploring, I skied back following exactly in my original tracks. I may be a slow learner, but I got the message right out there in the woods.

Lena gave me the story of her discussion with the village women. I never took that trip again, but I still may have occasionally done some dumb stuff. At least Henry didn't have to figure out what to do with my stiff frozen carcass. God is great.

We did witness the interesting, awesome breakup of the river's ice in the spring. Maybe you have read of the roar of four feet of ice breaking for a two thousand-mile trip. It is not that way. The ice breaks and surges with a whisper into huge blocks. Then the mighty currents jostle these blocks toward the sea. The blocks float and submerge and rise like whales from the other blocks as each block lunges for its own private space. That ended my ski trips.

Our next deployment in Alaska was at North Pole on the road system. North Pole is near Fairbanks on the trailing edge of the heart of the suburbs. Fairbanks is a full service city served by a railroad, a modern, commercial airport and a four lane highway. It is home to the highly regarded University of Alaska, Fairbanks. There is no way to get into remote wilderness predicaments here. Wrong.

The snow gets deep enough but not paralyzing deep. The Fahrenheit gets low, very low. Even so there are lots of fairly balmy winter days of thirty-five below and even warmer sometimes.

Lena cleverly located a full time job teaching school at Eielson Air Force Base. I craftily avoided full time employment in favor of finding more adventure for this essay. Never mind that twenty-two years have passed.

YUKON RENEWAL

I stood on the bank of the frozen
Yukon River in Western Alaska.
A small group of Indians and myself
Indians of the Holikachuk Band
It was late spring, almost summer
The river was still imprisoned by
an Arctic winter of ice Four
feet thick on the thin ice
Of unknown depth elsewhere,
but of thickness beyond
Reason to cut through to catch the fat sheefish or to
Harvest the valuable beaver.
Valuable for their meat and their
fur-opposing forces not
Withstanding as these hibernate
in their warm havens far to
The south in another time zone of a distant land.
Then the ice cracked and began to move
Not with a roar but with a soft sound even
more fierce than a roar; the ice broke.
The softness of the sound deceived
none of us for we knew
It came from 1000 miles of river ice.
Pushing with forces, awesome
beyond comprehension.

ADAM AND EVE FOR ATHEISTS

Sweeping itself and all in its path however sturdy it
might appear.
Downstream as water always flows,
toward the ocean- the
Bering Sea.
Cold beyond cold
We watched as the mighty ice
made its move through the
forests and tundra.
And for a short time we all turned
silent, each with his
and her own thoughts.
In my thought, I knew I was watch-
ing winter being washed
To the sea.
Now we would have summer.
For those who survive on the Yukon
summer is never taken
for granted.
There was no spring; sum-
mer was here; it will soon be
winter. More ice.

-Fred R. Kuester
Teaching Resident of Grayling, Alaska
Spring 1994

The Adventures
Near North Pole

I passed security clearance and was permitted to have a trap line on the Air Force base. Lena would teach all day. I would trap from a line that I worked on skis and snow shoes. I did most of the cooking and mopping. Luckily I never had to clean the toilet because I have never seen a toilet that was so dirty it needed cleaning. Because of my impeccable standards, it wasn't a bad situation.

I did have some unusual experiences in those forested hills. Some simple things can be scary and seem dangerous, although they are really laughable. Here is ones, there is a partridge-like bird called a Franklin's grouse or sometimes fool hen. I suppose they weigh about a pound. In the winter, they fly down into the snow where they bury themselves for the night. Supposedly that keeps them warm. I suppose if something has feathers, that can be an effective strategy. At times, I would walk on snow shoes to check my trap line in the dark. These birds had the hilarious habit of letting me get within about six feet from their little hidey hole, and then boiling out with a loud flutter of wings. It is pitch dark. It is utterly silent. I am walking on the deep snow and this great threatening sound disturbs the Arctic night about six feet from my face. It's kind of aggravating at first.

There is a waterway that drains from the base toward the Tanana River. The ice got up to four feet thick in some places and was thin in others. It seemed like I could walk on it anyplace, but this stream had some of the characteristics of the mighty Yukon. Underflow of water would erode the ice in sneaky places. At one of those, my feet became disassociated from my brain and I fell full length into water about one foot deep. There was no danger of drowning, but it was about forty below zero. It was only about a ten-minute hike to my pickup truck so this wasn't too scary. My clothes froze to ice instantly from my under wear to my heavy coat with the wolf hair ruff. This icy cloth clanked like a coat of iron mail as I waddled through two feet of snow to the truck. I was concerned as to whether I could bend the frozen knees of my pants so that I could operate the pedals. No problem. The knees bent. I drove home. A hot bath never felt better.

My next ice water education took place on the frozen Tanana River. This is a deep angry river in places. I was snowshoeing about fifteen feet from shore when I heard gurgle, gurgle, gurgle about three feet to my left. The water was open under a thin crust of snow. No, I didn't fall in. That could have been very serious. I was wearing long snowshoes with a long tail, but I managed to turn around in place and make a nervous trip to shore.

I have had many hundreds of hours on skis and snowshoes up the Lochsa River in Idaho and have never felt that I was in a dangerous situation except for driving on the icy road. I know the country. In Alaska, I was an untrained, uneducated pilgrim regarding the hazards. When leaving familiar country great caution is often required. God has looked after me, but there are limits. Again, it is written: "do not put God to the test."

The Christian Faith

Quote as I remember from Feynman, a famous physicist who died recently.

"Do not say, how can it be like that? because you will go down the drain into a blind alley from which no one has yet escaped."

I don't know the concept to which he was referring, but it seems appropriate here. Feynman was a very smart man.

Also, Albert Einstein was known to express his faith in the existence of a powerful God. Einstein was a very smart man. Without Einstein's insights, civilization as we know it would cease to function.

Most of us don't understand this stuff that was so clear in the minds of these gentlemen, but we accept their knowledge because it works. My point being that there is a lot of spiritual information that is beyond our comprehension. It is not fair to reject it because we see through the glass too darkly.

Throughout the span of the earth, people of most cultures have believed in an afterlife. They couldn't explain it but they believed it. Who knows where they got their information? No one knows, but it is fun to guess. As time passed, they developed theories about the nature of this afterlife and they invented knowledge. I'll work around that as we proceed to the wonderful, certain knowledge of Jesus Christ, our Lord and Savior.

To find God we must believe in some sort of an afterlife. Don't push it too hard. We don't know much about it. It is safe to assume that God is in charge of the afterlife; and Heaven, wherever that is, is his home. He wants to welcome us to his home because he is a loving, friendly God. He takes delight in his people (Psalms). St. Paul's letter to Timothy: he wants all people to be saved.

The next leap of faith after accepting the reality of an afterlife is: God is real.

Along comes Jesus who was the Spirit of God wrapped in a body that God provided for him. Jesus thanked him for that body. Jesus is a historical person. Historical means known to historians and written about. He was not conjured up out of peoples minds. This is elementary information to Christians.

But was he God? Is he still God? Yes he was God and still is God. This is proven by his murderous death and return to mortal life where he was seen by many. The death and resurrection are recorded primarily by men who wrote the New Testament. Some were eye witnesses. Twelve men who had nothing to be gained except the opportunity to be executed proclaimed the incredible message. These men did not care if they were killed for what they knew and told. Their only life purpose was to spread the Good News. The news they spread has stood the test of time for more than two thousand years. Such dedication does not come from fraudulent people. These were the first Christians. St. Paul of Tarsus came along a little later after his miraculous conversion to Christianity.

It is promised that we will be with Jesus, God, if we believe these facts. Jesus died. rose to life and lives in his heavenly home. I have avoided most specific scripture until now. Here is some scripture that cannot be avoided.

> For God so loved the World that he gave his only begotten Son that whosoever believes in him should not perish but have everlasting life. For God did not send his son into the World to condemn the World but that the World through him might be saved. He that believeth in him is not condemned but he that believeth not is condemned already. (John 3:16–18)

> The Father loveth the son and hath given all things into his hand. He that believeth on the son hath everlasting life and he that believeth not the son son shall not see life but the wrath of God abodeth in him. (John 3:35–36.

There are no such statements in the Hebrew Bible (Old Testament) referring specifically to Jesus. So how can the Hebrews know if they have not heard and they have not read? The Hebrew Bible does refer to a coming Messiah, but not to Jesus When Jesus did come he was rejected by the Jews of the time. He was murdered. There is no hope of personal salvation through Jesus in the Hebrew Bible.

St. Paul's letter to the Romans:

> That if you confess with your mouth the Lord Jesus and believe in your heart that God has raised him from the dead you will be saved. (Rom. 10: 9)

It couldn't be clearer. Therefore, if you believe the ancient stories of the Hebrew Bible are literally true or are allegories, there is nothing lost either way. Just don't push it on people. An allegory is a sparkling story with a deeper meaning. If you believe in Noah, that is okay. If your neighbor believes the story of Noah is an allegory, that is okay. Why argue about what neither of you can prove and what isn't worth a pinch of Pixie dust?

As a matter of interest, when many of the Jews were in semi-captivity in Babylon under Persian rule, King Cyrus offered freedom to return to Jerusalem for those who wanted to leave. But first, they needed a uniform doctrine. This was in the sixth century BC about six hundred years after Moses died. The Hebrews had different out looks among each other regarding the ancient scriptural beliefs. Ezra edited them into the version the Hebrews use today. Much of the Ezra version mirrors Babylonian history. Example: Gilgamesh. Also, Deuteronomy got edits into the second century AD. I am quoting things that I have read over the years.

I am not finding fault with Ezra even though he was a miserable jerk. There are tremendous messages in the old Hebrew traditions. That is why I started this essay with the Adam and Eve story. My take on the Hebrew Bible is believe what you want to believe. God will not be offended.

For direction and salvation refer to the New Testament. That is nearly all historical fact. Even the vision of John in the book of Revelation is the vision of a historical person. Never mind the 666, Revelation is filled with useful spiritual knowledge.

A little more clarification in the search for peace:

From the Hebrew Bible, we get the ancient people's search for knowledge that was unavailable at the time. Some of that knowledge has since been attained. Some examples are the age of the earth, the causes of diseases, the evolution of organisms, earthquakes, and eclipses. Did God kick in on this stuff? If so, then where? I don't know and neither do you, Neither does your Pastor. But I will heartily agree with any one who asserts that God has played some important roles. I just don't know what these roles are.

Scientists can prove the cause of many events that the ancient people could only guess at. But the ancients did know there was a God. I give them credit there.

If we deny the facts that the scientists can see with their very eyes, why should they pay much attention when we try to bring them the Gospel messages that are so precious to us? A final caution: be careful about judging the merits of the faith within the various Christian denominations. There are about 240 of them. All of them either reading the Bible differently or presenting the messages differently. All of them sincere. When push comes to hug, we are all united by our love and gratitude for our God(Christ) and by his love for us.

Do remember: if we judge others, then we will be judged by the same measure. What is that measuring stick? No one knows for certain. Everyone has an idea.

> The Lord bless thee and keep thee
> "The Lord make his face to shine upon thee and be gracious unto thee
> The Lord lift up his countenance upon thee and give thee peace"'
> (Num. 6:24–26)
> Jesus was and is The Prince of Peace.

Is There a Way that We Can All Get Along?

· ·

This essay began with the story of Adam and Eve to explore commonality among Christians and Atheists. We now examine the commonality between the various Christian denominations and even some of the commonality among Christians, Muslims and Jews. All the while we know there are some differences that cannot be bridged. Can these differences be tolerated?

As somewhat of a scientist, I am intrigued by a quote I read recently. I don't know who said it but he was spot on. As I recall, it went something like this, "When scientists recognize they have been wrong, they admit it and begin a new search for the truth. That is never the case in politics or religion." This resonated with me except for the word, "never." Scientists seldom use these words: 1) never 2) always 3) I am positive. Kind of aggravating sometimes, but they do tend to get along.

Science knowledge works like this:

1. Something looks true. This best guess is called a hypothesis.

2. The hypothesis is tested using observation, experiments and statistical analysis.

3. The work is examined, tested, reviewed, and duplicated by other scientists. If they get the same results, a theory is developed. If the work shows that an old theory was wrong or needs revision, then they have a new theory. A theory is not someone's best guess. It is regarded as a useable fact unless new information comes up. Theories don't change very often.

Regarding politics: It appears that truth versus untruth is not necessarily a criterion for integrity. Today, we are after integrity so we will skip politics.

When presenting the will or the nature of God, integrity must be a guiding light. The Holy Bible is our guiding light. So we of a particular denomination are positive that we have it right because we saw it in the Holy Bible. What we know cannot be altered or ignored. The conflict that crosses my mind is; if all of these sincere people have it right, then why do we have about 240 denominations in the United States? Since they are different from each other, at least 239 of them must have some little thing wrong.

Maybe one of them is absolutely correct in doctrine and presentation, but which one is perfect while hundreds are wrong? I'll declare odds of 239 to one that it isn't yours, but so what? For most of the differences, it doesn't matter what your outlook is or why your denomination is different. For a few items it might.

St. Paul wrote eloquently about the mystery of the Gospel. If parts of the Gospel were a mystery to one of the greatest Christians who ever lived, how can all things be crystal clear to us? Here are a few verses to help us doubt some of our long held views. We should never doubt the Divinity and the messages of Jesus Christ.

> For my thoughts are not your thoughts neither are your ways my ways, saith the Lord. For as the heavens are higher than the earth so are my ways higher than your ways and my thoughts than your thoughts. (Isa. 55:8–9)

Try this: Repeatedly, I am told that God is the same now, in the past, and forever. He never changes. That is certainly true as far as it goes. But consider this, does God recognize change?

"Separate yourselves from the peoples of the land and from the strange wives" (Ezra 10:11). In other words, become clannish and divorce your wives. I mentioned earlier that Ezra was a miserable jerk. A literal reader would read this as a direction for divorce.

Here is what Jesus said about that: "It has been said, 'Whosoever shall put away his wife let him give her a writing of divorcement. But I say unto you that whosoever shall put away his wife saving for the cause of fornication causes her to commiteth adultery'" (Matt. 5:31–32).

So much for never changing. Then again, this might be God's recognition of changing times or situations. What would he say now that situations have changed enormously? We could hassle this a long time and many people do but we won't.

> For what man knoweth the things of a man save the spirit of man which is in him? Even so the things of God knoweth no man but the Spirit of God. (1 Cor. 2:11)

> Now this I say that everyone of you saith, "I am of Paul and I of Apollis and I of Cephas and I of Christ. Is Christ divided? Was Paul crucified for you? Or were you baptized in the name of Paul?" (1 Cor. 1:12–13)

Were you readers baptized in the name of Luther, or of Calvin, or of some Pope? We are all brothers and sisters in Christ. Is there a way we can all get along? All 240 of us?

I don't want to do too much scripture however tempting it is. For every Bible verse, a man can quote, another equally sincere person can find and quote an equal and opposite scripture.

Earlier, it might appear that I came down a pretty hard on the Hebrew Bible. Let me clarify.

Scholars are almost unanimous in this observation. The Hebrew Bible is not a history book. It is a book of faith. It does have a lot of more or less accurate history, but that is not the intent of many of the ancient scriptures.

That is one of the reasons I started with the fascinating Adam and Eve story.

It is plainly not historically accurate based on timing alone, but in other ways also. God did not perform surgery on Adam while he was sleeping, slice out a spare rib, and create a gorgeous female. There are better ways to do that sort of thing, but males and females are closely linked in a process called marriage that makes them part of each other. That is nice, but there are difficulties. It has been written that men are from Mars and women are from Venus. Not true. We are not that close. If men are from Mars then women are, perhaps, from the elliptical of Pluto. I have this on good authority.

Sometimes, the old scriptures are based upon historical fact. I mentioned earlier that Ezra probably wrote much of the Old Testament during the time of the exile to Babylon. He produced a document that fit the needs of the Hebrew people in a particular situation at a particular time in history.

What about the Noah story that you have been waiting for? It effectively portrayed God's horrible punishment for sinners who strayed from his will. The people of the earth are not all descendants of Shem, Ham, and Japheth. Check the DNA and the archaeological evidence. At the time of the alleged flood, the entire earth was well populated with people. People have lived in North America for fifteen to twenty thousand years according to the latest evidence that I know of. That predates the timing of the flood. People, just like us, have been around for more than two hundred thousand years. The precise numbers are subject to change as the mass of data is further analyzed. People never walked with the dinosaurs. They missed that opportunity by more than sixty million years. There have been major floods in the Tigris and Euphrates valleys but never a worldwide flood.

Please don't fall into the trap of denial just because this might be new information to you. Those who deny are doing what I wrote about concerning denial a few paragraphs ago. Some of these myths are so strongly fixed in peoples minds that they cannot let them go. So what is the harm? There is nothing lost if you read for the message of faith and accept the story as a carrier of that message.

This is the loss if people persist in defending these stories as history: It is souls that are lost. They are lost for eternity. Perhaps, even destroyed in a Lake of Fire. Maybe. (Revelation 20), but definitely lost if our information is correct.

Lost because uncounted, but many people have rejected the entire Bible because they knew those early chapters of the Bible were not based upon any kind of history. There is plenty of science to prove this point. They never get to the story of Jesus, and it isn't their fault. It is the fault of those Christians who equate the belief and love of Christ with literal belief of the ancient, "undocumented stories." To become a Christian, they are instructed that every word of the Hebrew Bible is literally true.

We are the guilty ones. It is our fault. Those lost souls will cry and gnash their teeth because of us. It is time for us to feel sorrow and shame.

If you haven't figured it out by now, I'll tell you now this is personal to me. When I was a young man, my parents sent my sisters and me to church, but they wouldn't go themselves. Dad told me that when I got older, I would know better than what I was learning in church. This was in the 1940s. He knew that the scientific evidence proved the falsity of the literal readings in the Hebrew Bible. Regarding some scientific evidence, he said and I can recall the words precisely after more than 70 years, "This proves that everything in the Bible is false." He was fatally incorrect. Not his fault.

Dad said that when a person dies, he is buried in the ground and that is the end of him. The Sadducees also believed this. The Pharisees believed in an afterlife. They got their information from the same manuscript. Seventy or so years later, I still feel a little weepy for Dad. He was a good man.

Prayer: Please, God, in the precious name of Jesus, have mercy on my Father's soul even if I haven't found favor with you. Dad was a good man. We loved Dad. People gave him flawed information but he did send his children to hear your word. He did nothing to destroy anyone's faith.

So though I am writing this for atheists, I am even more praying that Christians will modify their approach to presenting the story of Jesus. His life, his status as God, his miracles, his resurrection, and his saving grace. Please do not link the saving message to the sparkling, ancient stories in the Hebrew Bible. Salvation is granted by the grace of God to those who worship the risen Christ as their personal Savior.

Regarding the fault of Christians including myself, I laid it on pretty heavy. Well it is heavy. But the fault does not so much lie with the people in the pews. We get our information from our pastors. The pastors have been well trained in presenting the word of the Lord in the appropriate manner commanded by the leaders of their denomination. So we believe them.

But their training has been lacking. They were trained in seminaries and Bible schools. How can the teachers and administrators in these schools not know that these ancient stories are myths? They have unlimited access to the relevant information, but they persist in imposing misinformation upon the minds of their young students.

Surely they are smart enough to recognize that many people will reject the risen Christ because of these professors' insistence that the history of the ancient stories be regarded as the inerrant word of God and therefore are literally factual. Is there a Satanic influence in their curriculum? That is a question I will not try to answer because I cannot read their hearts. Let them answer the question.

Abraham, Ishmael, and Isaac. Christians and Muslims and Jews

• •

Another opportunity to get some good out of the Hebrew Bible. We do have some common ground. Surely, there is a basis for us to get along and live in peace?

There is one huge commonality between Islam and Christianity. We worship the same God of Abraham. We call him God. They speak different languages. They call him Allah. There is one huge split between us. Muslims regard Jesus as a highly respected prophet. We, Christians, are convinced that Jesus is the earthly appearance of the almighty God. We both believe that Jesus still lives.

Consider the fact that Allah and God are different names for the same spirit. How did our differences come about?

Abraham's wife was named Sarah. Her female servant was named Hagar. Abraham and the servant girl produced a son. They named him Ishmael. Sarah and Hagar didn't particularly like each other. It didn't help that Ismael was Abraham's son.

In the supernatural course of events, Sarah and Abraham had a son. She named him Isaac. Isaac, Ishmael, and Abraham worshiped the same God.

Things got more testy around the Abraham-Sarah household. Sarah won this one. Hagar moved away taking Ishmael with her. Ishmael did not abandon his roots or his faith. He kept in touch with Abraham and Isaac. Abraham outlived Sarah and buried her. When Abraham died, Ishmael and Isaac worked together to bury their father near Sarah.

Ishmael and Isaac parted ways, still worshiping the same God, the same God of Abraham, Muslims, Christians, and Jews. Christians recognize God in three major manifestations—Father, Son, Holy Spirit. All the same. In fact, Jesus breathed on a man and said, "Receive the Spirit."

Now, consider our commonality with Jesus. Jesus claimed to be God. This was a common claim by the rulers of those times. But Jesus was the only one who could prove his claim. He was horribly murdered and then pierced with a spear. The murderers killed him twice over. He returned to human life and was seen by many.

He was more than a prophet. Prophets don't return to human life.

Isaiah portrayed the coming Messiah as "The Prince of Peace." Jesus never harmed anyone. He never killed anyone. He never wanted anyone to harm or kill people in his name. He never attempted to force anyone to be his follower. Everything was voluntary.

Accept him as the living God who will welcome you into his heavenly home. Love God, "Love your neighbors, love your enemies." Accept him as the living God who will welcome you into his heavenly home if you just say, "Yes, I believe." Do it today. There might not be a tomorrow.

Misconceptions
and Clarification

. . . .

Most Christians observe a festival meal called "Holy Communion." In the early days, Christians were murdered for this. They were regarded as pursuing a cannibal ceremony. Because of the words we use, it is not unreasonable that people would think that.

We eat bread. We call it the flesh of Jesus.

We drink wine or grape juice. We call it the blood of Jesus.

I have never met a Christian who took those words literally. I suppose there are those who do, but no one has ever said it to me. For my own denomination, this is a spiritual event. The bread and wine are just bread and wine. Within and under the bread and wine is the spiritual presence of God. Since God is present everywhere, that shouldn't be too much of a stretch.

Some denominations regard this bread and wine as representing the spirit of God. No cannibalism here. As reported to me, at least one major denomination claims the bread and wine become flesh and blood as they are digested. No problem here. Everything we eat becomes part of our body in one way or another. Even tripe and spinach. You may have my share.

It is a common misconception that we worship three gods: Father, Son, and Holy Spirit. I can see that people might think we worship multi-Gods but we don't. There is one God who presents himself in at least three magnificent forms. Plainly God is a spirit. "Jesus breathed on them and saith unto them. 'Receive ye the Holy Ghost'" (John 20: 22). Thus, God the Spirit emanating from God the Son. There should be no conflict here. Here are two supporting verses.

> God is a Spirit and they that Worship him must worship him in Spirit and in truth. (John 4:24)

> Now the Lord is that Spirit and where the Spirit of the Lord is, there is liberty. (2 Cor. 3:7)

We worship one God. Sometimes, we recognize his presence in the human body of Jesus. Sometimes, we are recognizing the fuller nature of our powerful God while always recognizing that he is a Spirit who can appear in any form he chooses.

Among the Christian denominations, we observe many differences of opinion regarding our understanding of the Holy Scriptures and their proper presentation. Our differences are not generally salvation related. They are peripheral to the certain message that there is an afterlife. Jesus is in charge of that afterlife.

Jesus Christ is Our Eternal Savior

North Pole, Alaska
Sometimes it snows.
Sometimes big company comes to town

FRED R. KUESTER

Lena's momma, Cuddle Cat, AKA Eagle Bait

Grampa Kuester, July 1991
The author's father to whom this book is
dedicated. A kindly old gentleman.
Fred Albert Kuester

Do not put God to the test
Stinky, the obviously happy cat at bath. Do not
try this at home. Those are the author's hands.

The young bald eagle that attacked
momma cat but was repulsed by Lena
wielding her protective broom.

Big Bill Mitchell with Babe the Holstein
heifer. Babe was one of his predictable girls.

My son William at age ten. 1973
He appears to be putting God to the test in the
Bitter Root Mountains of Northern Idaho. The
precarious situation was done with camera angle.

About the Author

I was raised in the suburbs pf Milwaukee, Wisconsin during the Great Depression. There was nothing great about it. I learned to hate at an early age. One of my early childhood memories was of the war in Europe. Why do these people hate each other? War meant guns and bombs. People killing each other.

One breakfast morning, Dad opened the Milwaukee Sentinel Newspaper and announced that we were at war. The carnage continued for four years and to this day. I am aware that nations must deploy a powerful military and that war cannot always be avoided, but I hate it. This has shaped my empathy for all suffering people. Everyone has a face.

I became a professional forester, courtesy of Michigan State University and Auburn University. I think much to the amazement of some professors. I never was a premier student. After a satisfying career, I retired, went back to school, and became a high school teacher, courtesy of Lewis Clark State College in Lewiston, Idaho. Two careers of service to the people of this nation..

I am now a retired octogenarian. That sounds like a disease, but it isn't. Although there are plenty of diseases that go with it. My wife, Lena, and I share a peaceful life on a rural home site in North Idaho. Except that I did feel a compelling urge to write this essay from a sense of gratitude toward Jesus Christ, who I honor as "The Prince of Peace."

CPSIA information can be obtained
at www.ICGtesting.com
Printed in the USA
LVOW11*0403211017
553257LV00002B/9/P